IF I DIE, PLEASE BRING CHEESECAKE TO MY FUNERAL

Donloree Hoffman

Copyright 2013 | DonloreEbooks
Edmonton
ISBN: 978-0-9879551-1-1
(trade paper)

© 2013 Donloree Hoffman. All rights reserved. This book is protected by the copyright laws of Canada. This book may not be copied or reprinted for commercial gain or profit.

DEDICATION

For my two biggest fans.

Mom.

Thank you for naming me Donloree and always laughing at my 'funniness and silliness.'

Jon.

Without you, I would not be who I am. Thank you for never letting me give up on my dreams, and doing anything and everything to make them happen.

TABLE OF CONTENTS

I Blame Angelina 1
An Apple a Day Keeps the Ambulance Away 3
New Things in the New Year 8
Popularity isn't as Grand as They Make it Out to Be 19
What's in a Name? 23
Starting Your Day Right 31
Red and Cream Zebra 34
Something Every Woman Needs .. 39
Honesty Really is the Best Policy . 44
It's All Greek to Me! 54
Not for the Faint of Heart 58
Ridiculous Rules 65
I Do Not Love Kayaking 72
Myth Busting 78
Confessions 79
About the Author 80

I BLAME ANGELINA

I have spent more of my life than I would like to admit, hoping and praying that Angelina Jolie would get a muffin top.

She has failed me in every way.

Even after giving birth, she still remains muffin top free. If she had a muffin top and embraced it, all women everywhere would be liberated.

My faith in Angelina to champion the everyday woman was so great that I decided to not be overly concerned about my muffin top. After all, the last thing I would want to be is out of fashion when the muffin top became the next big thing in haute couture.

To be ready for Angelina's show of daring, I consumed M&Ms, Doritos, white breads, and pastries on a regular basis, and also avoided strenuous exercise.

The muffin top has yet to make an appearance at New York Fashion

Week. After over a decade of waiting, I finally realized it was never going to happen.

It was time to liberate myself of wearing *foundational undergarments,* akin to a straight jacket, in order to fit into my clothes. What can I say? I think it's important to be able to breathe *and* sit down without looking like you've pulled every muscle in your back.

A woman can only wait so long for Angelina to come through for her before its time to change tactics.

It was time to get to get my arse to the gym.

AN APPLE A DAY KEEPS THE AMBULANCE AWAY

While thinking about how to combat my slower-than-a-slug metabolic rate, I had an epiphany. Why not hire an expert to help me get rid of the muffin top? Pure genius! I completed a good, old-fashioned Google search for '*Muffin Top Slayer.*' Poor results were returned.

Go figure.

After more sensible Googling, I found a personal trainer who fit my '*Muffin Top Slayer*' ideals and booked an appointment.

Before starting with a personal trainer, you are required to fill out a bunch of forms promising that you are healthy and will not sue the trainer if you die; which only makes you think you're about to die.

Then the assessment appointment comes, which involves measurements you never wanted to know, activities you can barely do, and a confessional of all your sedentary and dietary sins.

While discussing my current nutrition, or lack thereof, I was given a broad guideline to start with — eat real food.

If it's a fruit, a vegetable, or you can kill it, eat it.

Simple enough.

I immediately implemented the eating plan. I went home, baked some brownies, and *killed* them.

Then I felt guilty.

For the remaining three days leading up to the first training session, I followed the eating plan without fault. An hour before I left to get my muffin top's butt kicked, I consumed a heaping plate of spinach, bell peppers, cucumbers, tomatoes, and half an avocado.

Popeye would have been proud.

I went to the gym early so I could warm up to ensure medical help wouldn't be required to get me back home. The gym was colder than a meat locker. I kept my sweat pants and warm-up jacket on during my brisk jog. At the one-mile point on the run, I was on the verge of heat stroke. To keep from stroking out, I attempted to strip off the outer layer of clothing while continuing to run.

Word of advice: In order to avoid near-death experiences on the treadmill, press pause before taking off any warm-up clothing.

The training session kicked off with a circuit of weight lifting with sprints mixed in. I anxiously completed the first exercise and started to feel rather nauseated.

Then came the step-ups.

I was pouring sweat and we were only two minutes into the work out. On the last step-up, I started to see black dots and suddenly had to sit down.

Then I had to lie down.

The Muffin Top Slayer towered over me and looked rather concerned.

I looked quite pale…deathly pale.

I drank some water and tried to get a grip.

Muffin Top Slayer: *"Are you okay? Do you need some Gatorade? An ambulance? You look really pale.*

Donloree: *"I'm good. I just need a minute. GOSH. Apparently I am totally out of shape."*

Muffin Top Slayer: *"It's always eye-opening for people, but I am surprised, seeing how you do go to the gym somewhat regularly. What did you eat today?"*

Donloree: *"I ate really well. Heck, I even had a huge salad an hour ago."*

Muffin Top Slayer: *"Ahh...that's the problem. You should eat a piece of fruit before training. Here, eat my apple."*

I sheepishly ate the Gala while sitting on an exercise bike. The black spots started to dissipate and, five minutes later, I was a new woman. I completed the rest of the workout like a woman on a mission.

Another valuable lesson learned from the school of hard knocks: An apple a day keeps the ambulance away.

NEW THINGS IN THE NEW YEAR

I am absolutely sure a man invented skiing. I don't know many women who would decide to strap long boards to their feet, climb thousands of feet up a sheer mountainside, and then slide down as fast as possible, while trying to avoid trees, cliffs, and other natural speed bumps, with only two thin poles to assist them in not dying.

A few years ago, my husband and I went on a New Year's ski trip with his company to Kicking Horse Resort in Golden, BC. It was a last minute addition to our holidays, but it was free. I love free things, so I agreed after a few seconds of contemplation. I promptly went out and purchased new snow pants, gloves, ski socks, and a few other cold weather necessities, since I start to freeze whenever the temperature drops below -8 Celsius.

Honestly, it was a great excuse to go shopping.

We heard that snow blades were the way to go, so we each rented a pair on the mountain and strapped them on. Once we were ready to start skiing, I immediately had to go to the washroom. I started the hike across the lodge in my ski boots. All first-time skiers should be required to attend a class called *'Walking in Your Boots Without Making a Fool of Yourself.'* There is zero mobility from your big toe to your mid-calf, which makes it extremely difficult to not look ridiculous while walking. I clomped awkwardly and loudly across the lodge and nearly tumbled down the stairs three times before I reached the bottom.

Finally, we started skiing, or at least I thought we did. We started down a hill with about two degrees of incline, close to the ski lift. I started to scream and panic. My husband started to sigh. We saw a ski class in action 30 feet up the small slope. I laboriously side-stepped close enough to eavesdrop, until it became obvious I was doing everything they were doing, only 10 feet behind them. The ski instructor gave me a nasty glare, so I decided it was best to move on.

After a few more times down my *'practice hill'*, we started up the ski lift.

Why don't people explain things to you?

Do I look like a woman that knows what she is doing?

Ski lifts come equipped with safety bars that you are supposed to pull down so you don't fall off the lift while traveling up the side of a mountain. How are you supposed to know about this blessed safety feature if no one tells you? We traveled thousands of feet up the side of a mountain and hung hundreds of feet above the earth, wearing slippery pants without the safety bar in place. I wrapped my leg around the chair and clung onto the side rail for dear life, while trying to keep my poles and snow blades in my possession.

About halfway up the mountain, I made a comment about how a safety bar would make the ride up much less stressful. The worst part was when the lift stopped and then started to violently rock back and forth. We were a quick stop away from learning how to '*heli-ski*', and I definitely didn't want to learn that on my first real skiing adventure.

The last time I skied was when I was 14 years old with my youth group at Crystal Mountain. I kept to the bunny hill and rope tow. At the end of the day, I mustered up enough nerve to try a run, but ended up using my skis like a sled, sliding down the hill on my butt. Looking back now, I realize that day can't actually be classified as skiing. Everyone who heard that this was my first day of skiing grimaced, shook their heads and told me that Kicking Horse is an expert mountain. Then, each and everyone one of them wished me luck. Thanks. If there is one thing I am not, it's an expert skier.

Once we managed not to slip off the lift and arrived at the top of the Catamount lift, I had a full-blown panic attack. I suddenly realized I had to go down the hill on the boards I had happily strapped to my feet just an hour earlier. I desperately wanted to have a happy couple experience with my husband, so I tried to smile and to ski across the hill. It took me about 15 minutes of skiing back and forth, while trying to keep the panic at bay, to make about 300 feet of progress. My husband, who is from Saskatchewan (the flattest Province in Canada), patiently coached his stricken wife, who is from Washington (a mountainous region in America), on the finer points of how to ski without sliding face-first down the mountain. We continued our slow, very painful progress until we reached a section of the run that had a cliff off to the left, a rock wall on the right, and steep decline.

Without warning, I started to slide towards the cliff. In an act of complete desperation, I made a sharp turn towards the rock wall and lost every ounce of control. I did what any self-respecting woman would do — I screamed, threw my poles away, and fell over. Both of my ski blades flew off and I and started to shake uncontrollably from overwhelming fear. Hysterical sobbing then followed.

People we knew skied by and waved happily.

My husband convinced me that it was best to keep skiing, and that we couldn't stay at that location indefinitely, no matter how warm my newly purchased snow pants were. What actually got me to move were the snowboarders that kept jumping off the cliff above me and landing just inches away from me. There was no safe place on the mountain.

After what felt like an eternity, we finally reached a point where I could see the lodge…only a thousand feet to go. Earlier, I had thought this moment would be a happy one, but unfortunately for me, it was a steep section of the mountain and there was nowhere to go but straight down.

I completely lost it.

Tears of terror ran down my face and I started to sob uncontrollably. I decided the best course of action was to take off my skis and slide down the last thousand feet on my butt underneath the chair lift. After wrapping myself around one of the posts holding up the ski lift, I took off my skis and started to slide down the hill in my slippery pants. Skiers and snowboarders stopped to see what this crazy, sobbing woman was doing. Fortunately, once again, my sensible husband convinced me to put the skis back on, for safety reasons. When I reached the bottom of the hill after two hours of painstaking work that should have taken 30 minutes, I just sat in a snow bank and cried with relief. My husband just sat there bewildered.

We took a lunch-break and worked on getting me to be able to breathe normally.

Skiers are such friendly people. Normally, I would have enjoyed talking to the people visiting from all over the world. One woman asked how the skiing was and my response surprised even me. When I opened my mouth to talk, painful sobs poured out and I wept. She seemed to think that my boots were hurting my feet. I didn't correct her. It was less shameful than to admit I was deathly afraid of the mountain. I decided it was best not to talk to anyone, since I couldn't do it without crying. I kept my eyes on the ground and tried to overcome my fear.

After another hour or so, I decided to give it another try. After all, I'm not a quitter. The second attempt was a bit better. I didn't cry, even though I really wanted to, but I still couldn't stop without falling over. I missed some of the basics while eavesdropping on the skiing class earlier that morning. How is a woman supposed to know which ski is the downhill ski? I picked one of them to be the downhill ski, but I picked wrong. This would explain my inability to stop. If you put all your weight on the downhill ski, stopping is not an option; you just keep going straight down the mountain.

Straight to your death.

I am both tenacious and ridiculous, so I went up a third time. I remembered to breathe *and* use the safety bar on the lift. We had an hour to get down the mountain. It seemed reasonable since the previous run had been done in less than two hours.

Due to my mini panic attacks and falling over, it took longer than expected, and our departure time was looming. There was a distinct chance that we would miss the bus that would take us the 15 kilometers down the mountain back to our hotel. After such an epic day of skiing, the last thing I wanted to do was miss the bus ride to the hotel. We absolutely had to hurry and there was no choice but for me to go as fast as womanly possible down the steepest part of the mountain.

I nearly took out three small children and a snowboarder in my uncontrolled, screaming descent. The screaming notified the more advanced skiers of my arrival and they promptly got out of my way. When I arrived at the bottom of the hill, I enthusiastically ripped off my skis and happily gave them back to the rental shop.

We caught the bus just as it was ready to leave. I sunk into my seat, glad that I hadn't died during my first day of real skiing.

Let's be honest, skiing just isn't for me.

If these things happen to you, skiing may not the sport for you either:

- You break out into a cold sweat when you start to slide down a miniscule incline that isn't even part of the actual mountain.

- You ask the ski lift operator at the bottom of the hill if it's possible to take the lift back down if you are too afraid to ski down.

- When someone asks you how your day of skiing is going, you break down sobbing, unable to form proper sentences.

- Your equally inexperienced skiing partner starts to ski backwards, encouraging you to move towards him down the hill.

- It takes you five times longer than the average skier to go down the little green run.

- You find yourself sitting in a snowdrift, praying for the end of the world to come so you don't have to finish going down the mountain.

- The sorest parts of your body are your hands from their death grip the poles.

The next day when we woke to find 14 inches of fresh powder, I rode to the top of the mountain, sat by the fire, read, and drank lattes all afternoon.

I'm a chalet woman, what can I say?

POPULARITY ISN'T AS GRAND AS THEY MAKE IT OUT TO BE

I go to the gym every single day…even on my off-days. Yes, this is more than a bit OCD, but I am a creature of habit and enjoy the hot tub, steam room, and foam rolling. My showers at home don't need the soap scum removed, but do require a good dusting now and again.

I keep all my workout gear at the gym, so all I have to do is roll out of bed, eat breakfast, and brush my teeth before I head to the gym. One morning I went to grab my gear out of my cubby and my shoes were missing. Out of the corner of my eye, a piece of paper winked up from me from where my shoes should normally be found.

It was a note from a woman who took some shoes home that she thought might possibly be her shoes. She wasn't 100% sure, so she left a long diatribe about how she took some shoes and if she took your shoes, you should email her. She ended the letter with her email address and a drawing of a smiling flower.

At this point in the morning, I was not a smiling flower.

I found myself standing in the locker room, dressed and ready for action, but no shoes.

A huffy email was drafted from my phone, demanding she return my shoes ASAP.

They were returned the next day with a very apologetic note.

I promptly put my name on the inside of my shoes and made a public service announcement to all the women in the change room about the shoe thief.

A few weeks later, as I got dressed for a killer leg day, my shoes went missing. One minute my shoes were there, and then two minutes later they were not. At that moment, I was officially upset and unsure about the kind of women who train at my gym. While I got ready for work, after not working out because my shoes were MIA once again, I devised a plan.

I decided to go out and look at all the women's feet intending make a scene when I found the perpetrator. The pent-up angst from not being able to train my legs was going to be unleashed upon the shoe thief.

While applying my mascara and practicing my speech, I noticed one of my friends covertly motioning to me. She quietly let me know that a somewhat confused looking woman just walked in with shoes that looked just like mine.

I staged a confrontation.

I found the suspected shoe thief standing next to the shoe cubbyholes, looking bewildered. I put my hands on my hips, stomped over to her, and minced no words.

She indeed was wearing my shoes, simply because she couldn't find her shoes. They looked similar to her shoes, and since she didn't know where hers were, she opted to use mine…

...WITHOUT SOCKS!

The shoes were still warm when she handed them back to me.

The most incredulous part was that my shoes appeared to be about 3 sizes too large for her. She had to batten those suckers right down to get them to stay on, which resulted in a clownish appearance. I don't even know how she managed to keep them on while making them all sweaty, without wearing any socks.

I just have one question.

"Who are these women, and how do they not know what their shoes look like?"

Apparently, I have the most popular shoes at the gym.

I've always wanted to be popular, but if this is popularity, I think I'll pass.

WHAT'S IN A NAME?

My name is Donloree.

Just wait, it gets better. My maiden name was Donloree Dickau and I grew up in Puyallup.

Donloree Dickau from Puyallup.

Wow.

I love my name and have never wanted a different one. People tend to think '*Loree*' is my last name, especially over the phone. I am constantly explaining that it's all one name...one *big* first name.

My name gives people a stunned moment of shock when they first hear it. A look of confusion and a thought of, "*What the heck did she just say?*" runs across their face before they can cover it up. The look of panic always makes me laugh a little bit.

Despite how much I love my name, I do get frustrated with the questions that follow after I introduce myself to someone. Most people tell me it is *so unique* and proceed to ask me about the story behind my name.

This conversation would never happen to a woman named Sharon on her first day of work.

New co-worker – *"Hi there. It's great to finally meet you. My name is Fred. We're very excited to have you on board here at the office."*

Sharon – *"Thanks. I'm glad to be here."*

New co-worker – *"I've been meaning to ask you, where did you get such a beautiful name? There has got to be some story behind it. Did a man named Ron share something with your family around the time of your birth and your parents created the name "Sharon" because what Ron shared was so meaningful? Or something even better? Do tell! I can't wait to hear!"*

Sharon – *"Umm, no. My mom saw the name, really liked it, and so they named me Sharon. That's about it."*

New co-worker – *"Oh. I see."*

For a few years, I worked for the government. I like to refer to this time in my life as *'being paid to watch paint dry.'* A man named Roger who worked with me insisted on pronouncing my name, "*Dawn-Lori.*" His quirky pronunciation was noted by many people, but no matter how many times people told him the correct pronunciation of my name is "*Dawn-lah-ree,*" he continued to "*Dawn-Lori*" me.

This annoyed me to no end.

To make all things equal, I pronounced his name, *"Row-Ger".* Unfortunately, I never got up enough nerve to say it to his face.

During my time as a civil servant, working hard at not working, I purchased a bike. I noticed several brave souls biked to work with a suit in their backpack. They were fit, happy, and inspiring.

Who doesn't want to be fit, happy, and inspiring?

Every morning, I put on biking shorts, normal shorts, a cute tank top, and a light jacket. Office appropriate clothing was crammed into a backpack, along with my lunch, and I was off.

A few days into my newfound mode of transportation to work, I saw one of the fit, happy, and inspiring coworkers also enroute riding his bike. He was a few blocks ahead, so I biked like a mad woman to catch up.

I am a wee bit competitive, to say the least.

It was my third week of biking, and I wanted people to think I was amazing. He had been biking for years and was in great shape. Me?...not so much. I sucked wind and desperately tried to appear nonchalant about keeping up at the red lights.

Finally the office tower was in sight. I made it.

There is a hairpin turn 800 feet from the bike cages. My counterpart didn't decrease speed, gave a slight lean, and hopped the curb with ease.

I followed closely behind.

I leaned around the bend only to find my bike trembling from my rigid handling. Nonetheless, I did not slow down. I needed to keep up. The curb appeared with surprising speed, and suddenly, the world slowed down. It was as though I was underwater.

It was day 19 of biking and I had no idea how to hop a curb. I braked with all my might. The bike stopped abruptly, but I did not.

As I hurtled through the air, I said a little prayer.

"Dear God, please don't let anyone I know see me."

After barrel rolling and nearly taking out a newspaper stand, I ran back to my bike and grabbed it out of the street, right before a bus came by. Blood was pouring down my arm, but I didn't take notice. I needed to catch up to my coworker.

My brain said go, but my legs said stop.

Suddenly my legs gave out on me, and I fell into a heap next to the newspaper stand. Black spots crowded my vision and a trickle of sweat ran down the side of my face.

Breathe. Do not faint.

The next thing I remember is opening my eyes to find two kind men peering at me worriedly. As one of the gentlemen undid the strap on my helmet, I heard an ambulance siren in the distance.

Looking past the two concerned men, I saw a horseshoe of spectators encircled around me.

"Are you ok?"

"Did you crash your bike?"

"Do you need juice?"

"Are you hypoglycemic?"

"Did you hit your head?"

All my responses were crowded out by shame and confusion.

Luckily two EMTs arrived and kept me from having to answer the questions.

EMT – *"Hi. So, you crashed your bike, eh?"*

Donloree – (My right hand was still holding my bike in a death grip) *"I guess so. Wow. This is embarrassing."*

EMT – *"Nothing to be embarrassed about; it happens."*

Suddenly, my humor returned and an awkward laugh began to tumble out of me.

EMT – *"Do you know what day it is?*

Donloree – *"Yup, it is Tuesday. It is my 19th day of biking. You would really think I would be better at this by now. That darned curb. Wow."*

EMT – *"What is your name?"*

The laughter came in full force. I knew my name was about to become problematic.

Donloree – '*Of course. My name is Donloree."*

The two EMTs shared a concerned look.

My name and the uncontrollable laughter sealed my fate. I earned myself and my shiny new bike our very first ambulance ride, sirens and all. I insisted the bike come with me. After much cajoling, the EMT wedged the bike into the ambulance next to my gurney. For some reason, he didn't like the idea of just putting it on my lap.

By the time my boss tracked down my husband to notify him I was MIA, after being seen biking earlier in the morning, I had been diagnosed with a severe case of ridiculousness.

One part competitiveness, another part clumsiness, mixed together with a crazy name, leads to all sorts of epic adventures.

Unfortunately, this one wasn't covered by insurance.

STARTING YOUR DAY RIGHT

There are good mornings, and there are bad mornings.

A good morning involves strolling out onto a deck in Hawaii with a cappuccino in hand or waking up with the sun streaming down on your face as a gentle breeze wafts through your window while the birds serenade you awake.

A bad morning involves parking at the gym, grabbing your workout gear, quickly hopping out, and locking the door to your car, only to realize that your car is rolling backwards towards a BMW. Not only is it is moving without you in it; it is picking up speed at an alarming rate.

At this point in the bad morning, a complete awakening happens. All of the synapses are firing at once, and words you wouldn't repeat in public start flowing out of your mouth.

I threw down my workout gear and tried to open the car door to no avail.

Somehow, in the midst of the stress, I noticed that the back door of the car was unlocked. In 2.5 seconds, I came up with a plan to jump in the back seat, hurl my body over the consul, and try to find the brake in time. Luckily, the executive function in my brain decided to kick in as well.

I grabbed my purse and dug for my keys while chasing the car down. The car was moving very quickly at this point. I threw my purse down, contents flying everywhere, and unlocked the car door. I was able to grab the e-brake and bring the car to a stop before an unfortunate meeting with the BMW.

I stuck the keys into the ignition and quickly drove it back into the stall it had rolled out of, so the three cars queued up to park could go by. With shame and shaky legs that could barely hold me upright, I meekly gathered the contents of my purse that were now strewn about the gym parking lot.

Suddenly, I was more awake than if I had drank eight espressos in a row. It's

not a good way to start the morning, but
it's a sure fire way to wake up in a hurry.

RED AND CREAM ZEBRA

One day I hope to be a decent runner. I want to pass people while racing, instead of memorizing what all the other runners look like from behind.

A few winters ago, I joined a hardcore running club in order to help me on my quest to become a better runner. We met Tuesdays and Thursdays right after work in the river valley. The coach was the peppiest, in-shape woman I had ever met.

She cheerfully devised workouts that involved running up and down large hills. As if running hills wasn't enough of a workout, she had also had us do sprints, speed work, and high knees while running them. Each week, after an hour of running all over the river valley, we met back at a community league to do core exercises, such as the plank.

Just in case you were wondering, I hate the plank.

I live in the subarctic of Canada, which means there were some days that even very peppy, in-shape people won't run up and down hills as fast as they possibly can due to dangerous conditions.

Running class was *never* canceled. We still met in snow, ice, freezing rain, or blizzard. Even in the -40 degree Celsius weather, we could be found running up something. When things got icy, we adapted, and still showed up to get our butts kicked. On one of these snowy, very cold days, our coach planned a workout that involved over 1,000 stairs, simply because the stairs weren't icy.

I managed all the stairs and felt the very bottom of my lungs for the first time in my life. There was also an odd wheezing noise that came out whenever I reached the top of the Hotel MacDonald stairs.

I usually hate doing the core exercises, but after that workout, I was happy to do any exercise that involved lying on the floor. As we were finishing up with the plank, I saw my husband poke his head into the room. He came to pick me up with surprise tickets for an event that started in 15 minutes. I quickly changed back into my work clothes, tried to make semblance out of my now salty, sweaty hair, swiped on some mascara, and off we went to the conference center.

My legs were quickly turning into Jell-O from the stair sprints.

The event started at 7 pm, and we didn't leave the running group until 6:55, so we were obviously quite late. Once we got into the conference center, we started quickly down the many escalators to reach our event. The second set of escalators is ridiculously long, and on our hurried jog down the moving stairs, I fell.

I went flying forward and found myself sliding head first, face-down, on the supremely long escalator with my laptop bag leading the way. My husband grabbed my ankle to end my slide towards certain death.

While laying head first, face-down, all I could think about was my hair getting sucked down the side of the escalator and getting stuck at the bottom, with the stairs continuously hitting me in the face.

It is ironic what you remember when you think you're about to die.

Suddenly, I recalled a frightening story my grandma told me about a little boy getting his foot sucked down the side of an escalator while she watched in horror. I didn't want my whole body to get sucked down the side of the escalator, so I rolled awkwardly toward the middle, still going down headfirst. I was so tired and frightened that I all I could do was meekly say, *"Help, help, help…"*

My husband quickly came to my rescue, jumping over my body that was strewn over most of the escalator, and hefted me right-side up. He saved me riding the rest of the way down headfirst and arriving at the bottom like a beached whale in front of important people wearing nice suits.

I had ripped holes in my best pair of pants and received huge stair marks up the right side of my body. I was a red and cream zebra.

Once I could breathe normally and realized I was going to live, I was suddenly very thankful to be running late. If we had been on time, who knows what tragic thing would have happened.

Are you familiar with the domino theory?

After all of this, I applied some lip-gloss, and we continued on to the event — ripped pants, stripes, and all. I was there already, why not rock the disheveled red and cream zebra look?

Exactly.

I managed to run up and down 1,000 icy stairs without incident, apparently that 1,001st stair is a doozey.

SOMETHING EVERY WOMAN NEEDS

Every Tuesday and Thursday morning, I run with several women out of the gym downtown at 6 am, if it's warmer than -20 degrees Celsius.

Every Tuesday and Thursday morning, my alarm goes off at 5:17 am.

Every Tuesday and Thursday morning, I press snooze twice and am late for the early morning run.

Every Tuesday and Thursday morning, I get dressed in my work clothes, throw the cold-weather running outfit in my gym bag, and run out the door with a granola bar in hand.

Every Tuesday and Thursday morning, the running women are forced to wait three to eight minutes for me to quickly change into my running outfit and grab a drink of water. The running women are very nice. They have never said anything about my propensity towards lateness, although it must be severely annoying. I know this because I annoy myself almost every Tuesday and Thursday morning.

If you annoy yourself, it must be pretty bad.

So, I came up with a plan to stop annoying the running women. I laid out all my running clothes and put my work outfit, shoes, and accessories in a very cute green tote bag. I was *not* going to make anyone wait for me this day. Nope. I was organized.

I got up at 5:27 after pressing the snooze button once, drank a tall glass of water, had a multi-vitamin, and took some time to make toast. I was able to have such a leisurely morning because I was just so organized. Everyone was pleasantly surprised at the lack of a crazed wardrobe change this particular morning.

After surviving the early morning run, I grabbed my cute green gym bag and pulled out my work outfit to get dressed for the huge day that loomed ahead.

While getting dressed and chatting with the other women, I suddenly had a small moment of panic. Did I remember everything I needed for the day? What if I forgot something?

Sometimes I decide to indulge in Obsessive Compulsive Disorder fears, which on this day meant I had to dump out all the contents and see what was missing.

To my absolute horror, something *was* missing. Something that every girl needs. Something that is non-negotiable.

I forgot my bra.

There are times in my life when I can't keep the panic to myself and I announce my latest fiasco to everyone. This was one of those moments. Suddenly, all of the women in the change room knew of my current crisis.

Donloree – *"Oh…my…gosh! I decided to be prepared and very organized last night. But I was so organized that I didn't put my bra in my bag. How is that* *even possible? A girl needs a bra in her day! My gracious."*

Huge pause in the change room

Donloree – *"Well, I guess I'll just have to go home and get my bra. Nothing like being late for work. What am I going to I tell them…that I forgot my bra? All the men in the office would really like that one! Can you just imagine how that conversation would go? 'Hey there. It's Donloree here. Yup, I am just running late, need to go home to grab my bra…hope to be in around 9:00.' "*

After many unhelpful suggestions, including to just go without a bra, there was an actual, albeit unexpected, strange solution.

Cathleen – *"Do you want to borrow a bra? I have an extra in here."*

Donloree – *"Uh…no, that's ok. I mean, it's kind of weird, don't you think?"*

Cathleen – *"No, not at all. I have a ton of extra things in here for such an occasion. The worst thing to forget is* *your pants. Now, there's something you absolutely can't go without!"*

I took a quick look at the clock and saw that it was 7:58. I had to be in work in 32 minutes and still didn't have a bra to wear.

The braless situation was getting dire.

Donloree – *"Ok...only if you are sure, and it's not totally weird."*

Cathleen – *"Nope, here you go. Just give it back on Thursday. Remember, there was that one day I forgot pants, now that was quite the day!"*

All the women laughed as I gave Cathleen the '*Most Prepared Running Woman in all of History'* award. Despite my hesitation, I put the bra on, hardly filling it out, and called it a morning.

A woman's got to do what a woman's got to do to get to work on time.

HONESTY REALLY IS THE BEST POLICY

A few years ago, during the dark and frigid winter months in Edmonton, I resolved to lose some weight and drop a couple dress sizes so I could possibly wear a bathing suit without cringing, once summer rolled around.

I hate running outside in the -30 degree Celsius weather, so I got a membership at the community league in our neighborhood and started swimming in the evenings. It was a great workout, and didn't require me to wear all my cold-weather gear at the same time.

People started asking questions.

"What are you training for?"

My mouth opened and what came out shocked even me. *"Umm...a triathlon."*

Apparently I was ashamed about my desire to wear size 8 pants, and, besides, completing a triathlon sounded *so* much better. Before I knew what was happening, most of my friends and family heard I was going to compete in a triathlon

I found myself cross-training, weight-lifting, and completing workouts that involved swimming, biking, and running. That's the thing with words, once they are out there, you can't get them back.

So, I decided to go for it.

After all, how hard could it actually be?

The big day was smack dab in the middle of summer, and it arrived, sunny and full of promise. I arrived, grouchy and full of fear. I braided my hair, donned my Speedo swimsuit and biking/running outfit, and begrudgingly got in the car.

Upon arrival, I encountered hundreds of spandex-clad people excitedly jumping around and stretching. I went directly to the tent to pick up my race package and have a strange man use the biggest sharpie I've ever seen in my life to write my race number, 803, on my calves and arms.

What had I gotten myself into?

After being branded, we were herded, like cattle, down to the waterfront where an announcement was made about the lake being infested with leeches. My stomach was already queasy, and the toast that I had for breakfast threatened to come up, as unexplainable fear gripped my heart. I started to look for an escape route, but ducking under the pylons and running at top speed past my husband and best friend would probably be noticed. I tried to breathe while I waited for the race to start.

When the starting gun finally went off, all of the women aged 24 to 29 ran towards the leech-infested water as though their lives depended on it. After avoiding being trampled, I jogged cautiously towards the waterfront and dove into the shallow lake. The water boiled with body parts, and, after a near kick to the head and getting a bird's eye view of a very large armpit, I decided to hold back.

I waited in the ankle deep, leech-infested silt for the crazed athletic women to swim by me before I started up again.

To my immediate dismay, I couldn't see a darn thing in the water.

It was like sticking your head into a bowl of chocolate pudding. Panic set in, and I started to doggie paddle while my mind feverishly worked out a solution. I started to hear a high-pitched whine and then realized, I was the one making the noise. I was officially hyperventilating and even the doggie paddle was too much. I didn't want to be disqualified, so I employed a panic inspired back float. While looking up into the sky, wondering what the world I was going to do, the heads of two men in a canoe came into my view.

Two Men in a Canoe: *"Miss, are you okay? Would you like us to help you?"*

Donloree: (awkwardly treading the waist deep water) *"YES! But* *wait! Does that mean I am disqualified?"*

Two Men in a Canoe: *"Well, yes...but if you're struggling, perhaps we should take you out."*

Donloree: (tears starting to fill up my goggles) *"I have worked so hard to get here! I have to finish. I have to keep going. Can you row next to me, just to make sure I don't die?"*

Two Men in a Canoe: *"Umm, there are a lot more people in the race, and we have to watch all of them. Hmm. We can check on you later, though."*

Donloree: (in a wobbly voice) *"Okay, that would be nice. Thank you."*

Two Men in a Canoe: *"And by the way, you're floating off course. You're going to want to go that way."*

The longest swim of my life ensued.

Battling panic and hyperventilation, as well as being lapped by a group of men swimmers, took every single ounce of energy I had. My husband and best friend were forced to watch a floundering woman use a doggie paddle and back float method to complete a swim that took six times longer than it should have.

When I finally emerged victorious from the leech-infested, waist-deep lake, I could barely walk. There were three canoes filled with men paddling alongside of me, cheering me on. That was the most cheerleaders I have ever had for one of the most embarrassing moments of my life.

I hobbled over to the transition area to get ready for the bike. Most people pull on shorts and get biking. I plopped to the ground, ate a granola bar, and drank a ton of water.

I was just relieved to be alive.

The hilly bike ride was surprisingly uneventful. I made good time and even passed some people. It felt reassuring not to require any supervision to complete this leg of the race.

I entered the run tired, but the finish line was visible. The realization that I was actually going to live through this adventure invigorated me. Much to the surprise of my athletic husband, I took off sprinting. He was impressed by my sudden energy, and he decided to run alongside of me and interview me on video to get my thoughts while I was in the moment. His focus was completely on interviewing me, and not the obstacles on the sidelines. A head-on collision with a stop sign occurred and he went down. Blood was coming from his temple and the medical team was called.

I just kept running.

What was I supposed to do? I had already lost 40 minutes in the swim, I didn't want to lose more time in the run. I decided he would understand.

Before I knew it, he was bandaged up and running alongside of me again.

Crossing the finish line was one of the most glorious feelings in the world. I conquered a huge feat and lived to tell about it. Sure, there was no one else crossing the finish line with me, but who cares? I finished.

We enjoyed the rest of the hot summer day and watched the professional tri-athletes complete the course. Oddly enough, none of them used the special *'Donloree Method'* to complete the swim.

That evening I used a strong soap to wash the '803' off my arms and calves. Within about three seconds of scrubbing, it became quite obvious I should have applied waterproof sunscreen that morning.

I was VERY burnt.

Did you know that sharpies are the equivalent of SPF 80 sunscreen? *'803'* was branded into both of my upper arms and calves. Due to the way they wrote the numbers, it actually looked more like *'BOB'* than *'803.'*

The stiffness in my legs, especially my left leg, was intense after the race. The next morning I could barely walk. When

I tried to get out of bed, I fell over and confirmed that 74 dust bunnies live under my bed. I was unable to put my left heel on the ground, and my calf was the size of a small basketball.

It didn't seem like normal triathlon wear and tear, so off to the hospital I went.

I hopped into the ER and waited.

The waiting lasted six hours, while random people with even more random illnesses came in. A few even came in with buckets of specimens to show the admitting clerk, in an effort to gain quicker access to a doctor. I looked away and hoped they would go away.

There was concern that I had a blood clot, so I was sent for an ultrasound. Have I mentioned how ticklish I am? Screaming out in painful laughter while an ultrasound tech shoves an ultrasound wand into your hip joint is frowned upon. It was either laugh or cry, so I opted to laugh, and laugh quite loudly.

Due to my big mouth, I got crutches, a cast, a torn calf muscle, and a summer of strangers asking me, *"Who's Bob?"*

I learned the hard way how important it is to tell the truth, even if the answer is as ridiculous as '*size 8 pants.*'

IT'S ALL GREEK TO ME!

Sun salutations, warrior pose, downward dog, and tree pose sound like items from a fantasy novel, not a fitness class.

Yoga is a completely different language.

If you tell me to get into a warrior pose, followed by a shooting bow, and then finish it off by saluting the sun, you might as well be speaking Greek. I have no idea what to do, nor can I even start to bend in the ways required to complete randomly named exercises.

Learning a second language is supposed to assist you in becoming a cultured and well-rounded individual, so I decided to give yoga a try.

Upon entering the studio, I was greeted by several calm, bendy people wearing very tight clothing. I suddenly felt like the chubby girl who tries out for cheerleading — awkward, out of place, and not sure what to do next.

While clutching a Pilates mat to my chest, I noticed the bendy people were gathering yoga supplies of blocks, mats, blankets, pillows, cords, and bolsters from a cart on the wall. This was my first real yoga class, no one told me I needed to bring along a yoga checklist.

Luckily the instructor noticed my anxious stare and grabbed all the necessary supplies for me.

Then the torture began.

She had us bend like circus contortionists, and then told us to rest our head lightly on the floor in front of us. I was already bending as far as womanly possible and my head was a good two feet from even coming close to the floor. It was so absurd that I started to giggle. Intuitively, I had a sense that laughing in the calm, unhurried space of yoga class would be unacceptable, so I desperately tried to hold it in. Unfortunately, the laughter came out in pressured bursts with large amounts of spit.

My uncontrollable giggling was not appreciated. I quickly sobered up by thinking about sad things, like never being able to eat chocolate again.

She instructed us to do completely impossible things while saying all manner of words with more vowels than consonants, and at least 12 syllables.

Due to my lack of fluency in the yoga language, I covertly watched to see what the rest of the class did, and desperately tried to mimic their movements.

At the end of class, we did some final stretches to *'completely loosen up'* all our tight muscles. She led us through a stretch that involved putting your left foot on your right knee, bending into a squat, leaning forward, and then merely doing a handstand to deepen the stretch.

Simple…right?

I couldn't get past step two in the task. There was no way a pretzel handstand was up next. There are only so many times a woman should risk her life doing stupid things, and this was not one of those times.

Yoga is for masochists.

It's an hour-and-a-half of doing torturous things that are impossible for this woman.

All I can see gaining from yoga is more character, and I've got enough of that to last a lifetime.

I'm saying no to pretzel handstands.

NOT FOR THE FAINT OF HEART

There are two different kinds of *"once in a lifetime experiences."* One is a cherished experience that is held close for a lifetime, such as going to the Taj Mahal, seeing the pyramids, or meeting your hero. The other is anything, but cherished. The second kind of experience is an event in your life you desperately pray will never happen again. In fact you go out of your way to make sure it never, ever happens again. You commit whatever resources, time, and energy it takes to ensure that it remains a *'once-in-a-lifetime experience.'*

Step aerobics has become a once-in-a-lifetime experience for me.

My neighbor invited me to go to the local gym with her to spend our evening in a step aerobics class. She promised the class was beginner friendly and easy for everyone, and that people of all levels of fitness were welcome. With her vow of a good time in my back pocket, I grabbed my Nikes and sweat pants and we were on our way.

I followed her with blind faith and abandonment. She had no fear of taking me with her…what a naive woman.

Upon arrival, I immediately noticed that I was severely out of place. Everyone else knew each other, and no one offered their gift of friendship to me. Perhaps it was because I was wearing oversized sweat pants and a vintage Ronald McDonald t-shirt that I got eons ago. I didn't get the memo about the fashionable attire required for step aerobics. I held back, hoping the class would start soon.

Suddenly, the gym fell silent as the lithe instructor, fully clad in spandex, walked in. She shouted in a very excited voice to the class, *"Good evening everyone! Please, come and pick out your step and l..e..t..'s g...e...t STARTED!"* While she bounced around at the front, I headed over to pick out a step.

Who knew there were choices?

I was late getting to the step selection location and the only step left was very large and extremely purple. This step was the mother of all steps — a monstrous step. I think that André the Giant is the only person that could have used this step with ease.

I had no other choice but to use André's step and fervently pray God would miraculously lengthen my legs. By the time that I realized the mammoth purple step was my only choice, the rest of the class was already in position, ready to follow the spandex poster girl to better fitness.

I started to hurry towards the back of the class with my step in tow. Apparently I was going too quickly for the gym floor, because suddenly a speed bump appeared out of nowhere.

I promptly tripped and started to hurl towards the earth. I panicked, let go of my huge step, and screamed for help. I had no idea a purple step could make so much noise.

After standing up and retrieving the step from hell, I meekly walked towards the back of the class, hoping to become anonymous. Unfortunately, that was no longer an option. The whole class had turned, wide-eyed, to watch my progress with the gym floor.

I humbly took my position in the back row.

Even the instructor seemed at a loss for what to do next. Apparently, it is quite uncouth to throw your step across the gym floor and fall over screaming prior to the start to class. I should have realized that this was only the beginning of losing all my dignity.

After the instructor recovered from her shock, the class got underway. "*Kick! One, two, three, over the box! Whee!!*" she announced, while leaping over her step, hands gracefully flying in the air. As I attempted to leap over the step, my hands flew into the air as well, but it was anything but graceful. No matter how I stepped, leapt, or turned, I was never with the class.

Most of my time in class was spent running circles around the step, trying to get on the correct side, only to realize that the whole class had moved over the other side of the step. A dog chasing its tail would have made more progress than I did that evening.

At the end of class, I was merely dizzy and embarrassed.

The next week when my friend wanted me to go to class with her again, I was somehow too busy to attend.

Every person who is new to step aerobics should be required to pass a clumsiness assessment test prior to enrolling in the class.

It would be simple. Take the test before the start of class and if you score a five or more out of six, you would be unable to participate.

Clumsiness Assessment Test

Please answer '*Yes*' or '*No*' to the following questions. Receive 1 point for '*Yes*' answers and zero points for '*No*' answers.

1. Have you ever tripped over something non-existent in public? (e.g., a crack in the sidewalk)

2. Is your purse a menace to all displays in department stores and needs to be checked at the door?

3. Do you have a history of tripping up escalators?

4. Have you ever lost your shoes and tripped over a curb while crossing the street at a busy intersection downtown, and inadvertently stopped traffic?

5. Would people you know well be concerned about your personal safety if you picked up a new sport due to your past clumsiness history?

6. Do you blurt out ridiculous comments at least once a day that you wish you could cram back into your face once they've been said?

0 – 1 Points – Step Freely! Book yourself in as many step aerobics classes as you want and flaunt your coordination to everyone else in the class.

2 – 3 Points – Step Cautiously. Try one class and see what happens. It is unlikely that you will be cursed with a step aerobics mishap, but give special care and consideration while in class.

4 – 5 Points – Step Fearfully. Be afraid of what may possibly happen if you go to a step aerobics class. There is a 17.49386% chance that nothing crazy will happen to you, but do you really want to risk it?

6 Points – Don't Step! We are twins separated at birth! Avoid all group exercise classes — they are a threat to your health and the health of others.

RIDICULOUS RULES

Most Christmases my family goes bowling at least once over the holidays. For some reason, it is a family tradition to pay money to wear someone else's shoes and throw balls at wobbly pins.

Bowling is fun, but rather ridiculous for several reasons.

Reason #1

You have to rent shoes. When you go bowling you *must* to wear shoes that 8,000 other people have worn, that are still warm and a bit gooey from the disinfectant that was just sprayed in the shoe. Why? What are my non-marking tennis shoes going to do out there in bowling land? Not only do you have to wear the horrible shoes, but you also have to pay the bowling alley to wear them.

It just doesn't add up.

Reason #2

There are way too many rules regarding the wooden floor area that makes up the bowling lanes.

Above every lane a sign is posted that reads, *"Do Not Cross White Line."*

What is going to happen if you step across the line? Is there a secret infrared light that detects when even a toe has broken the rule? Does a silent alarm go off and the bowling police come escort you out of the bowling alley? It is completely over the top.

Nor can you have food in the bowling area.

If you want a snack, you have to sit 20 feet away from your friends. Eating people are segregated from the non-eaters. If you want to share a plate of nachos with someone, you must notify them when you're leaving the snacking area to go bowling so they can supervise the snack. The notification process usually involves bellowing loud enough so that people three lanes over can hear.

"Hey Frank, FRANK! I am up next, do you want any of these nachos?"

It's important to notify your friends when you are leaving the snack post, lest the server comes to take your nachos away.

Reason #3

The whole point of the game is to huck a heavy rock straight down a very long strip of hard wood to knock down the ten pins (or five pins, depending what country you're in) all at once. I have a feeling this sport was created about 300 years ago in a small village somewhere.

So, there we all were, the whole family, with our rented clown shoes on and bowling balls in hand. We began throwing our bowling balls down the long lane with much hilarity.

At the age of thirteen, I got over the fear of sticking my fingers in the dark, unknown bowling ball holes and began to throw the ball like most normal people. No longer was I relegated to walking up to the white line, bending over at the waist and rolling the ball down the lane with a good heave-ho!

On this particular day, I was bowling with confidence. I grabbed my ten-pound purple and green psychedelic colored ball, took a few confident strides and tossed the ball down the lane with flair.

My husband, sportsperson extraordinaire, is always telling me how important it is to follow through when playing sports. I could hear his patient voice in my head and continued my forward stride after releasing the ball. Then, unbeknownst to me, my right foot crossed that sacred white line of the bowling lane only to be followed by my left.

Suddenly it was as though I was on ice skates.

The bowling people had the lane waxed to a high sheen and my rented clown shoes were no match for glass-like surface. My follow-through was now pushing me forward, down the bowling lane, towards the pins. I was unable to get any footing and was tripping forward from the immense momentum my follow-through created.

I made a split-second decision to lean backwards in an effort counteract the forward momentum and stop the crazed, head-first careening down the bowling lane.

Sometimes the quick decisions made in life aren't always the best ones. In my panic, I over-compensated on mid-flight correction. I ended up going straight backwards onto my butt with my head cracking the bowling lane a split second later. It happened so fast that my arms didn't have a chance to catch my fall.

Most people didn't notice the deafening noise my head made on the lane because it was the exact sound of a dropped bowling ball.

Once I stopped seeing stars, I opened my eyes to see my whole family peering down at me in complete horror and shock.

My body was strewn across the bowling lane, a solid eight feet from the white line. I remained horizontal, unable to move from both pain and embarrassment.

Darn follow through!

The craziness of the situation hit me and I started laughing uncontrollably. The pain radiating from my head and the large amount of wax on the lane made my attempts to stand up futile.

In order to move the laughing woman off the lane, my family decided to push me down the lane on my butt. As I was being slid to my seat, I noticed ten lanes of people had stopped bowling to watch my latest fiasco. A panicked bowling alley employee ran over in a tizzy and started yelling something about calling an ambulance. In between my laughter and shame, I assured her that I was okay and to cancel the 911 call. She seemed relieved, mostly because she realized I wasn't going to sue the bowling alley. What would I sue for? Allowing ridiculous and clumsy people such as myself into the bowling alley?

The next day when I could barely move my neck from the whiplash I received while bowling, all I could see in my mind's eye was that sign mocking me:

"Do Not Cross White Line"

No kidding.

Who knew not following this rule would cause such pain?

My new motto in life: *"Do what the sign says, no matter how ridiculous it seems!"*

I DO NOT LOVE KAYAKING

Many people start things, stop them, and start them again.

Myself included.

Heck, I have a partially knitted sweater still *'in progress'* from Christmas 2009. It has been so left for so long that I am going to have to start over because by now I am most likely knitting the wrong size.

In the very wise words of my mom, *"The road to hell is paved with good intentions."*

Or in my case, half-knitted projects.

The problem with stopping is, when you start again, you don't always get to pick up where you left off.

One of the activities I started, stopped, and hope to never, ever start again was an attempt to spend time with my husband while doing something he enjoyed.

Good wives kayak.

We signed up for an introductory class that started in a swimming pool and eventually made its way to the North Saskatchewan River.

Have I mentioned that I loathe boats?

I am deathly afraid of boats. If you ever hear panicked screaming coming from a canoe in the middle of a completely calm lake, I am in the boat. I would prefer to swim across a lake than get in a boat to cross it.

In my opinion, sitting in a boat is the same as *'Meeting Jesus face-to-face.'*

On the first day of class, happy, boat loving, people wearing neoprene, shook my hand while the arms of their wetsuits wildly flopped around their knees. I felt out of place in my tankini.

Each class had an instructional portion and a practical portion.

During the instructional time, we learned about things like the biomechanics of rolling your kayak, keeping your food dry while on the river, and how to avoid being trapped by a *'death machine'* in white water. Wet peanut butter and jam sandwiches are something a woman can overcome, but a '*death machine*'?

I did not feel reassured.

The practical portions were done in the pool. Once I was strapped into the extremely small kayak, I promptly began to sweat right through the neoprene skirt. Luckily, the sweat was quickly washed away by my first *'how to roll your kayak'* lesson.

Everyone in the class had rolled their kayak, moved on to practicing paddling techniques, and were enjoying the class.

I was unable to loosen my death grip from the sides of the kayak while bobbing up and down in the shallow end of the pool. Short, forced breaths kept bursting through my lips while I tried to convince myself to go for it.

By this time, I had earned a one-on-one lesson with one of the instructors.

After 25 minutes of coaxing, head shaking, and avoiding, she just flipped my boat.

Thank goodness, someone created an easy-to-find loop so I could quickly pull the release hatch on the *'skirt'* and avoid dying a very wet and upside down kind of death.

Did you know that unless you have gills, breathing under water is impossible?

I rewarded her act of daring with a strangle hold and spluttering screams that most likely left her partially deaf in her right ear.

I swallowed half that pool the first night of class.

By the fourth class, the panic attacks in the change room were lessening and I stopped drinking most of the pool. Finally, we graduated to the real world and took our kayaks out to the North Saskatchewan River.

I fasted and prayed for God to send me an epic illness the night before class. My fervent prayers went unanswered.

There was no reason not to go to class, other than cowardice, so I arrived with my neoprene on ready to meet Jesus face-to-face.

I sat in the kayak and screamed as the current took me down river.

Some important lessons were learned that night.

Lesson #1
If you just sit there and complain, you are at the mercy of the current. For pity sake, put your paddle in the river.

Lesson #2
Paddling up river is hard work. You have to be stronger than the current to make any gains.

Lesson #3
As soon as you stop paddling, you begin to lose ground. Whatever you do, don't stop paddling.

Lesson #4
No one appreciates a screamer.

Lesson #5
If boats make you hyperventilate, whitewater kayaking isn't the smartest idea. Do something you love.

I returned my boat to the head kayaker and went to find my knitting needles. I had a sweater to finish.

MYTH BUSTING

The women on the cover of magazines aren't that fabulously fat free in real life. All their cellulite, muffin tops, flabby arms, dimples, and imperfections have been airbrushed away into oblivion.

It isn't real.

On the other hand, cheesecake is real and fabulous. So have a slice, not just a sliver, and enjoy the journey called life.

Fulfillment and joy comes from living out your life's purpose and being who you are, even if it means you ride in an ambulance, nearly fall off a ski lift, or scream bloody murder while drifting down river on a kayak.

Live, love yourself, and laugh. Life is too short to obsess over a dress size.

And eat some cheesecake!

CONFESSIONS

I dislike running immensely.

Sometimes I drive over the speed limit.

My name really is Donloree.

Cheesecake, chocolate, and peanut butter are my kryptonite.

If I can't beat 'em, I buy cute shoes.

I truly hate static cling.

I bring large purses to weddings, just in case the favors are chocolate and there are extras lying around at the end of the night.

Sometimes I daydream what it would be like to be normal, then I fall asleep from sheer boredom.

If you tell me you can eat whatever you want and stay slim, I won't like you.

All of the events in this book actually happened.

ABOUT THE AUTHOR

I have been known to go about life without reading instructions. In my not-so-humble opinion, it is the most sensible way to get things done. The instruction manual is consulted only in dire situations, which are most likely a direct result from not reading instructions in the first place.

I realize this a rather unique approach to life.

I attract ridiculous and crazy adventures. While still in *utero*, my mom tripped and ended up rolling down a somewhat large cliff at a beach on the west coast. We both shook it off like champs, but random things have been happening to me ever since.

Over a decade of my life was spent pursuing the *'dream job and dream life.'* After working my way up the corporate ladder and living the life everyone else wanted, I came to realize that I wasn't living at all. Finally, I admitted I wanted more out of life, so I went on an epic journey from being overweight and unhappy to healthy and fulfilled, and started to live with purpose and passion. My greatest discovery was that I am better than I thought I was, and so are you.

I love shoving people off the cliff of possibility and watching them fly.

Along with being a leadership coach, speaker and author, my proudest accomplishments include working with Mother Teresa's Missionaries of Charity in Calcutta, competing in a Figure Competition, and renovating our first home.

"Do not follow where the path may lead. Go instead where there is no path and leave a trail."

~ Ralph Waldo Emerson

I would love to connect with you.

    Twitter: @donloree

    Blog: www.donloree.com

    Email: dl@donloree.com

www.ingramcontent.com/pod-product-compliance
Lightning Source LLC
Chambersburg PA
CBHW061500040426
42450CB00008B/1433